GOOGLE PIXEL PRO USER GUIDE (2022 EDITION)

A Complete User Manual for Beginners to Use and Master the Google Pixel 6 Series: Including Troubleshooting Hacks, Tips, and Tricks

By
Nath Jones

Table of content
INTRODUCTION 11

CHAPTER 1 15

Top Features..15

Design and colors 21

Tensor Chip 22

Camera specifications and features 26

What's In the Box 33

Specifications 33

CHAPTER 2..39

How to set up your Google Pixel 6 device 39

How to transfer data from an Android phone to a Pixel. 43

How to transfer data from an iPhone to a Pixel..48

How to transfer iCloud images and videos to Google photos.....................................51

How to make a request for the transfer of your videos and pictures.........................55

How to transfer data from a blackberry or Windows phone to a Pixel 58

CHAPTER 3..59

Start Your Device....................................59

Charge your Pixel phone 59

How To Reboot.......................................60

Using a Nano SIM Card..........................62

Make Use Of E-sim.................................63

Connect to Wi-Fi networks on your Pixel phone 64

How To Make The Most Of Wi-fi...........66

How to connect to mobile networks on a Pixel phone..68

Modify the setup of the mobile network 68

How to use your Pixel 6 phone with any mobile carrier 69

Acquire and use a sim-unlocked phone .69

Possessing a sim-locked phone 70

Resolve issues linked with the removal of a sim lock...71

How to use dual Sims on your Google Pixel phone..72

How to place a sim card into the phone while it is switched off. 73

CHAPTER 4..75

Getting around on your Pixel phone......75

Quickly change settings on your Pixel phone 75

3

Add, remove or move a setting 76

How to Take a Screenshot Or Record Your Screen On Your Google Pixel Phone 78

Using your Pixel 6 to take a snapshot of the current screen and preserve it 79

How to identify share and edit a Google Pixel screenshot.....................................79

How to access all of your screenshot screen captures......................................80

How to translate a screenshot correctly on your Pixel 6 device................................80

How to record your Google's Pixels screen 81

Create printouts from applications........82

CHAPTER 5 85

How to customize your device 85

Change wallpaper on your Pixel phone .85

How to customize the grid on the home screen 86

Add apps, shortcuts, and widgets to your home screen 89

Monitor screen and display settings on a Pixel phone..90

Visibility configuration..........................91

4

Modify the language 92

CHAPTER 6 93

Manage screen time with digital wellbeing 93

Have driving mode turn on automatically on your Pixel phone 94

Establish a driving policy in your Pixel phone 95

How to make contactless payments with your Pixel phone 95

NFC activation (near field communication) 98

Disabling contactless transaction 99

Find and set up devices near you 99

Allow or disallow notification 100

Resolve configuration issues with devices 101

CHAPTER 7 102

Use gestures on your Pixel phone 102

Activate or Deactivate gestures 103

Get the most from your Pixel phone battery 103

Restriction of apps that consume battery 106

5

How to make Use of less mobile data with data saver 107

How to change your screen color at night on a Pixel phone 107

How to change your screen to night light or amber automatically 108

CHAPTER 8 109

How to make and receive phone calls..109

Accept or decline a phone call 110

Check your voicemail 110

How to enable transcription or voicemails 111

Activate donation for voicemail transcription...111

How to change call settings 112

Modify the volume and vibration settings 112

Modify the text responses....................112

How to block a contact/number 113

How to use caller ID & spam Protection 113

Disable or enable caller ID and spam prevention 114

Enable caller identification announcement 114

How to block and unblock a phone number 115

How to screen your calls before answering them 116

Where is call screen accessible 117

How to use other apps while on call 117

How to utilize picture in picture mode 117

Use Google assistant to make calls on your mobile device. 118

How to use direct my call 118

How to activate or deactivate direct my calls 119

CHAPTER 9 120

How to add new contacts from a group conversation to your contact list 120

Modify individual notification settings 120

Send and receive text messages in messages 121

How to send photos videos or voice recordings in messages 121

How to Provide your location information 122

CHAPTER 10 123

How to use applications on your device 123

How to download applications on your device 123

Download appropriate apps from third-party sources 124

How to alter the app setting 124

Automatically deactivate unused app permissions 125

How to disable or get rid of apps on your device 125

How to disable any Program that came pre-installed on your Pixel 6 device 126

CHAPTER 11 127

How to Protect your device 127

How to find your device 127

Ascertain the location of your smartphone 128

How to enable the find my device feature 128

Locate, lock or delete a lost or stolen Pixel device 129

How to lock and unlock your device 129

Configure screen lock on your Pixel 6 device 130

How to unlock your Pixel 6 device using your fingerprint 131

Use your face to log into apps and confirm payment 132

How to delete all facial information 134

How to disable the facial unlocking feature 134

How to keep your phone unlocked 135

Deactivate Smart lock 136

CHAPTER 12 137

How to change your settings 137

Activate quick Settings 137

Turn on or off settings 137

Add, delete, or reposition a setting 138

How to add or remove Google and other accounts on your device 140

Connect your phone to a Google or other account 141

How to delete, switch or add users 142

Remove any Google or other third-party account from your phone 143

Remove or change users 143

9

Change to guest mode on your device .144

How to create a backup of your Pixel phone's data or restore it 145

Activate or deactivate automatic backup 145

How to back up, restore data and phone settings 146

How to restore an account from a previous phone to a newly reset phone 146

How to manage the location settings on your Pixel phone 147

Turn on or off your phone's location accuracy 147

How to make your phone conduct a search for nearby networks or devices. 148

How to activate or deactivate the emergency location service 148

How the emergency locator service functions 149

Notification and interruption settings . 149

Quickly disable or enable interruptions 149

CHAPTER 13 151

Troubleshooting Your Device 151

INTRODUCTION

The Pixel 6 and Pixel 6 Pro are no doubt cutting-edge Google devices set to disrupt the smartphone industry. It's built completely differently to learn and adapt to you in so many ways.

The revolutionary Google Tensor is the heart of the Pixel 6 and 6 Pro devices. It is Google's first chip and it has a Processor capable of powering the smartphone. It also comes with an adaptive battery intuitive enough to know where you need power and send it there, and it lasts beyond 24 hours so you can experience an amazing adventure as long as you want.

On Pixel 6, you are the design inspiration. With custom color only drawn directly from your photos; your home screen finally feels like home.

You can choose when apps access your camera and mic and turn them off whenever you want.

No matter where you're traveling, live translation will be there for you. It is the world's most fluent phone and can translate your messages as you type. You can also translate pictures and words spoken aloud all without the internet.

The Pixel 6 and 6 Pro was built to respect darker skin tones by photographing them exactly as they look; authentically and beautifully. This makes it the most inclusive camera on a smartphone face.
Face un-blur makes your photos clear and crisp. You can snap silky-smooth long exposure shots with the Motion

mode, and with Ultra-wide selfies you can capture your entire crew. And the Magic Eraser feature removes all distractions in your image.

It's like a photo studio on a phone.

And with up to 20x Super Res Zoom on the Pixel 6 Pro you can get close...like real close.

The Pixel 6 is highly rated for its security so your digital life is covered. With Google's security Hub all your security settings are in one place that means your personal digital life is not shared with anyone.

The Pixel 6 and 6 Pro is a phone built with Google Tensor but personalized by you.

You've already got yourself an exceptional device. Now to learn how to use it maximally, keep readying this user guide as we explore and provide you with step-by-step directions.

CHAPTER 1

Top Features

Aside from Google's bespoke Tensor Chip, the Pixel 6 comes with much more new features that makes using the Pixel 6 series an amazing experience.

- **Camera**

The Pixel 6 series will come with a massive upgrade in their camera.

Both series will come with a quarter of an inch sensor. This sensor will be able to capture 150 percent more light compared to the previous Pixel.

That means the pair will capture details and colors in images more accurately.

The rear now comes with an ultrawide and the selfie camera comes with an ultrawide lens.

Aside from this, Google has also baked exciting features like the Magic Eraser, Face Un-blur and Motion Mode.

With the magic eraser, you can remove any distraction in the background of your image by just tapping your screen.

With motion mode, you don't have to go through the trouble of adding motion to your picture. It will add it by itself. Face un-blur just like the name implies, un-blur your face.

Furthermore, the Pixel 6 series camera now has a real-tone. That means the white balance; algorithm and exposure have been turned. Photos will now work for everyone, irrespective of skin tone.

- **New Design interface**

Another feature the Pixel 6 series comes with is a new design.
On the selfie camera, there is a centered hole punch and the rear camera now has a bar.

The bar is a design statement used to differentiate between the series from other Android smartphones. The series also comes in new captivating colors that have fancy names.

- **Fast Charging**

Google bumped up the charging speed of the Pixel 6 series phones by 30W; which is a major increase from its previous 18W.

Google claims that with this new charging speed, your device can charge up to 50% in just 30 minutes.

- **Scratch Resistance**

The Pixel 6 series has a larger display. This will give you more room when watching videos and performing other tasks.

Along with the display, the Corning's Gorilla Glass Victus comes with twice as much scratch resistance compared to the previous versions.

- **A Bigger Battery**

Not having enough on-screen time was a major issue with the previous Pixel versions.

As an improvement, the Pixel series now have better bigger batteries.

Batteries that Promise you longer screen time and battery life.

This new battery will enable more screen time, and according to Google the Tensor chip makes the Pixel 6 series consume less battery whilst performing intensive tasks.

- **Software Support**

The Pixel 6 series has now set a new standard in terms of software update.

The Google Pixel 6 series will continue receiving security and major updates till 2026.

This is a huge scale and it will impact the life cycles of Android devices for a long time.

In comparison to other Android smartphones, this is the best.

- **Live Translation**

The Pixel 6 series comes with the live translate feature and will translate your text as you type.

It is also integrated into other apps, meaning that you can easily translate texts in your WhatsApp, Snapchat, or Messenger app.

The best part of this is that you don't need an internet connection, you can easily translate offline. You can accurately translate text in French, German, Italian, Japanese, Portuguese, or Spanish, fully offline. Plus, it can also translate YouTube videos, podcasts, and more in captions.

Design and colors

The Pixel 6 series boast of a new design interface and colors. On the selfie camera, there is a centered hole punch and the rear camera now has a bar.

The bar is a design statement used to differentiate between the series from other Android smartphones. The series also comes in new captivating colors that have fancy names.

The Pixel 6 is black along the frames and has a matte finish. It comes in three colors, sorta seafoam, stormy black, and coral (almost pink)

Unlike its first edition, the 6 Pro has a polished frame but it also comes in 3 colors; stormy black, cloudy white, and almost sorta sunny.

Tensor Chip

One of the biggest changes in the Pixel series is that the Pixel 6 and Pixel 6 Pro will be powered by Google's first bespoke chip; the Tensor Chip.

Google explains that the Tensor chip is based on the future of machine learning and not where it is at the present.

The tents or cheap without consuming more energy will perform more intensive AI tasks more accurately and effectively.

The tensor chips since it's based on years of research gives the Pixel 6 exclusive and unique features.

The CPU setup is unique as it differs from chips because it uses a 2+2+4 configuration.

With the inclusion of 2 cores, the performance of the Tensor chip will be 2x more than other Android SOc.

Google designed the chip to be a premium system on chip; meaning that it will deliver effective, deliver the best of performance and security

The tensor chip will give the Pixel 6 am edge over other devices; it will perform more accurate task and consume less energy

For example, the Pixel 6 will use the most accurate automatic speech recognition model

Thanks to the new live translation feature the Pixel 6 and 6 Pro comes with, you can communicate easily with anyone who doesn't speak your language.

It goes further to enable this feature in your chat apps. That means you can translate messages right from your WhatsApp or Messenger apps.

And you can do all this without consuming your battery compared to the previous models

With the tensor, Google Pixel video can now match up to quality.

The Pixel 6 will now deliver videos with accuracy and vivid colors

It will also detect faces accurately and still consume less battery power.

The tensor chip also protects your user data and prevents attacks like voltage glitch, and electromagnetic analysis.

With the tensor chip you have access to real world experience at your fingertip.

Camera specifications and features

One of the best reasons to get a Pixel smartphone is always the camera tech and for the Pixel 6 series Google has gone all out with its upgrades.

First up you have Google's fresh new tensor chipset with its built-in isp for faster and more energy efficient image Processing and Google has also completely overhauled the camera hardware for the Pixel 6 series as well.

So, you get a 50-megaPixel primary sensor, that's two and a half times bigger than that of the Pixel 5. Google is no longer relying just on software smarts for those really nice-looking low light shots and that's all on top of a bevy of new features for shooting and editing great looking pictures on the go.

You'll notice that when any app starts using the camera you will get a little notification flash up top as well as a green dot that appears full time in that top right corner. On top of that inside the camera app you'll also get a shortcut to either save your

photos to your gallery as usual or stash them away in a password-Protected secure folder which is definitely handy for those more private pictures

The Pixel 6 and the Pixel 6 Pro's 50-megaPixel primary shooter boasts optical image stabilization and it can spit out impressively natural looking photos any time of day.

Google has spent a lot of time making sure that the Pixel phones can capture accurate colors and skin tones in any kind of light rather than boosting them to make scenes look artificially vibrant.

The night sight feature now automatically activates whenever the Lighting is a bit low but you can turn off that setting if you want to.

One of the fresh new camera features that Google has chucked into the Pixel 6 series of smartphones are in motion mode. It's action pan adds an aesthetic blur to the background for moving subjects while keeping them mostly sharp
although if your subject is running by other humans they'll have the same effect applied to them more often than not.

Another feature is the exposure mode, which is handy if you want to take a snap of a waterfall or cars moving at night. At any point you can quickly switch to the Pixel 6 or Pixel 6 Pro's 12-megapixel ultra-wide-angle lens if you need to fit more into frame and the good news is that this shooter can still Produce natural looking pictures for the majority of situations with reduced edge distortion compared with many rivals.

With a quick tap and by pinching in you can boost your camera all the way up to seven times digital zoom. At the two times zoom level your Pixel will still look clean and sharp.

However, in its first major deviation the Pixel 6 Pro serves up a 48-megapixel telephoto shooter with four times optical zoom so if you want to snap from afar this is a huge improvement at the maximum 20 times super res zoom.

Both Pixel 6 phones can shoot up to 4k resolution video at either 30
or 60 frames per second. You don't have to manually activate it either unlike with most rivals the Pixel 6 can automatically capture good looking footage when there is strong contrast.

The audio comes through clear; colors appear natural and stabilization is beautifully smooth even at top resolution.

The Pixel 6 Pro upgrades the selfie camera to a 11.1-megaPixel selfie shooter with a slightly wider angle for cramming more heads or background action.

The actual quality is basically the same as the Pixel 6. Although the Pixel 6 Pro can shoot video at a mighty 4k resolution using the selfie cam unlike the standard Pixel 6 which tops off at full HD resolution.

So, if you're into a bit of vloging then you might be more tempted by the Pro.

If you want to edit your picture and share them online or one of the other new features that Google has added into the Pixel 6 series of smartphones is the magic eraser tool and it's pretty wonderful.

This clever feature can automatically identify any distractions in your shot and then get rid of them in a jiffy and with quite remarkable results as well.

It is certainly a lot better than similar features on other smartphones although it can't work miracles.

You can erase any stuff that doesn't please you and poof it off.

What's In the Box

Here are the basic things you should expect in your Google Pixel 6/6 Pro device.

- The Smartphone
- Sim tool
- USB C to USB C charging cable
- Quick switch adaptor
- Screen Protector

Specifications

GOOGLE PIXEL 6

SCREEN

6.4-inch AMOLED

Ratio 20:9

FullHD+ at 2,400 x 1,080

90Hz Refresh

HDR10+

Gorilla Glass Victus

PROCESSOR
Google Tensor 2.8GHz
GPU Mali G78 MP10

VERSIONS
8GB/128GB
8GB/256GB

REAR CAMERAS
Main: 50 megapixels f/1.85 OIS
Wide: 12 megapixels f/2.2
Dual LED flash

FRONTAL CAMERA
8 megapixels

BATTERY
4,600 mAh
30W fast
charging 21W wireless
charging Reverse wireless charging

SYSTEM

Android 12

CONNECTIVITY

Dual SIM (eSIM)

Wi-Fi 6E

Bluetooth 5.2

GPS

NFC

USB type C

DIMENSIONS AND WEIGHT

158.6 x 74.8 x 8.9 millimeters

210 grams

OTHERS

On-screen fingerprint reader

IP68 certification against dust and water

GOOGLE PIXEL 6 PRO

DIMENSIONS AND WEIGHT

163.9 x 75.8 x 8.9mm

210g

SCREEN

6.71 inches

AMOLED LTPO

120Hz

1440x3120 Pixels

19.5:9

Gorilla Glass Victus

PROCESSOR

Google Tensor

INTERNAL MEMORY

128GB

256GB

512GB

RAM

12GB

BATTERY
5,000mAh

30W

REAR CAMERA
50MP

48MP

12MP

FRONT CAMERA
11.1MP

SOFTWARE
Android 12

Pixel UI

OTHERS
Fingerprint reader under the screen

Titan Chip M2

5 years of updates

CHAPTER 2

How to set up your Google Pixel 6 device

Setup your device

In this section, I'll be showing you how to set up your Google Pixel 6 or 6 Pro devices.

- First, turn on your device.
- On the first screen, you will be presented with a welcome note. Underneath are two options; language and assistive options.
- Go ahead and click on the language option to set your preferred language.
- You can also click on the assistive options to set up vision or hearing settings, etc.

- The next step is to connect to a mobile network. For you to do this you need to insert your SIM card or connect to an ethernet connection.
- Press skip if you are not ready to insert your SIM yet and connect to a Wi-Fi network so that you can get the latest software update.
- If you choose to not insert a sim card right now nor connect to your wi-fi, you won't see the option to log into your Google account throughout the setup Process. And additionally, the date and time probably won't be set automatically or correctly.
- Once your Wi-Fi network is connected, wait for the phone to get ready. It may take a few minutes.

- The next page will ask you if you want to copy data from your previous phone.
- If you have an old Android phone, you can go ahead and press Next. If not, don't copy.
- On the next page, you will need to sign in to your Gmail account. You can go ahead and fill in your login information or press skip to do it later.
- The next page will Google services options like; use location, allow scanning, send usage data, etc. Each of these is optional, so turn on or off any option you prefer. Then tap on accept.
- Accept the additional legal terms on the next page to Proceed.
- The next option will be to set your pin - a four-digit passcode. I

advise that you set it up now, don't skip it. Type in your passcode; something you can easily remember. It's going to ask you to type it again after you press next.

- Go ahead and retype your passcode. Then click on Confirm.
- Next, it will ask you to set up your fingerprint. Click on "No, thanks" to set it up later or tap "I agree" to Proceed.
- Click on start and then place your fingers on the sensor till it vibrates. Touch and hold until the circle is completely blue. Once done, you can add another fingerprint or click Next.
- The next step is to review additional apps. A list of apps will appear, you can select the ones

you don't want or just click "OK" to have them all downloaded to your phone.
- A tutorial will pop up on the next page. You can go ahead and skip it or try it out. It will show you how to navigate through the phone.
- Once it's through, click on Done. On the next screen, it will ask you to swipe up to go home. Go ahead and swipe.
- Now your phone is ready for use.

How to transfer data from an Android phone to a Pixel

If you have gone through the setup Process without copying your data, then the first thing you're going
to want to do is reset your

phone to go back to that initial startup screen.

- Swipe down from your home screen.
- Then swipe down again and hit on the settings icon.
- Scroll down to the system and tap on it, then scroll all the way down to where it says reset options.
- Click it and then Tap Erase all data (factory reset). It's going to ask if you are sure you want to do this as it's going to erase all of your data - music, photos, everything.
- Click on yes then type in your 4-digit passcode. It's going to prompt you one more time. Click on "yes erase all data". Immediately, it's going to start factory resetting your phone.

- Wait for a few minutes for it to reset.
- It will take you the initial setup for the Pixel device.
- Follow the setup Process above till you get to the copy data and apps screen.
- Tap Next, and click on next again on the next screen.
- To transfer your data, you need an appropriate cable that you will plug into both phones. Fortunately, Google will Provide you with everything you need to move all your data from your old phone in the packaging box.
- It comes with a C-to-C cable and a little converter, if you are not using an Android phone with a type c port. All you need to do is connect your cable to the

converter and you can connect each end to the phone.
- Once you've plugged them in, it will automatically see that there's a device connected and it knows that you're trying to transfer data.
- Your Pixel device will tell you to check your other phone. Your old phone will show a screen telling you to Copy your data to your new phone.
- Click on copy and it will ask you for your pin. It will take a bit of time to scan your old phone for any of the data that you have on it.
- Once it's done, it will be presented to you on your new phone and it will ask you what you want to copy.

- You will see the gigabytes of data available and it will also list out; apps, contacts, photos and videos, music, text messages, and pretty much all of the options that you can copy to your new phone.
- Select or deselect the little checkboxes if you want to copy or not. You can also tap on an option to see its list and you can go ahead and select or deselect anyone you don't need anymore.
- After making your selections go ahead and tap copy.
- So, while that's all happening in the background you can just go ahead and go through the initial setup wizard as usual.
- Follow the steps above to set up. Once you are done with the setup,

47

it will return to the copy data screen. Wait for it to finish copying.
- Once done, the next screen will tell you that your phone is almost ready. Disable the cable from both phones.
- Then click on done and wait for it to load then swipe up to do your home screen from the next page.

How to transfer data from an iPhone to a Pixel

If you use an iPhone device, follow these instructions;
- Follow steps 1 to 7 in the above section.
- Now, plug your iPhone lightning cable into one end of the little adapter that comes in the Pixel

retail box then plug the other end into your Pixel phone.

- Unlock your phone and tell it to trust your Pixel by tapping the trust button on the pop-up that appears.
- Once that's done it'll be connected. As soon as they're connected, sign in to your Google account. If you have a 2-step verification setup you'll need to go through those steps as usual.
- Click on the Next button and the Pixel will search the iPhone for all the data that it can transfer. It will take a few minutes then you'll see a spinning sync icon in the status bar on your iPhone.
- As soon as you've gone through that Process, you'll get a list of all the items you can copy from your

iPhone and you can select which ones you want. They include contacts, calendars, messages, attachments, pictures, videos, and music. Basically, anything stored locally on the phone.

- Once you confirm what you want to copy, click on copy and let it transfer everything in the background while you set up the rest of your phone settings.
- Once you are done with the setup, wait a few more minutes as all the information and media is copied across.
- Then you'll get a final screen telling you what has been copied and then you can go to your home screen.

How to transfer iCloud images and videos to Google photos

You can use Google's free backup and sync utility which is both for Windows and Mac to transfer your iCloud images and videos.

All you need to do is to download the tool directly from Google photos by clicking on utilities and backup from your computer. For Mac Users, you'll need to ensure all your photos held in the iCloud are being synced with your computer to do this.

- Go to preferences in the Photos app and click on the iCloud icon there. Ensure that the radio button to download originals to this mac is selected. This ensures a complete copy of all your

photos held both in the cloud and on the computer.
- Follow the usual installation Process to install backup and sync.
- Once installed, open the app and log into your Google account.
- You'll be asked what you want to do and tick the option to backup photos and videos. To speed things up, disable everything else except uploading your photo library.
- You can opt to choose between high and original quality. High simply means that Google will compress your images and reduce videos down to 1080p. Whereas originals remain unaltered.
- Click start to begin the synchronization Process. You can

monitor the Progress by clicking on the icon in the menu bar but do be patient because it can take some time.

For Windows Users, the Process is much the same however you should download the iCloud app which will copy all of your photos to your pictures folder before uploading
them to Google.

- Download the iCloud app from the Microsoft store.
- Once installed, log in using your apple account and choose which folders you wish to sync. Just select photos or videos and click apply.

- When you open your picture folder you will see a copy of your photos beginning to sync.
- Install Google's backup and sync app and log in to your Google account again.
- Then select your pictures folder just like the Mac. You can choose whether to upload in high or original quality and then hit start. Google will start the synchronization Process and if you switch back to Google photos you will see your photos beginning to transfer from the iCloud via your pc into the Google photos app.

How to make a request for the transfer of your videos and pictures

There are a couple of ways to transfer your iCloud photos to Google photos if you simply wish to do a one-off bulk transfer. Apple has a neat little service for doing just that which strangely is tucked away in their privacy website.

However, it can take up to seven days for Apple to complete the transfer depending on the amount of data you have.

- Simply navigate to privacy.apple.com and log into your apple account.
- Once logged in click on request to transfer a copy of your data. The next screen will display how many photos and videos you have

stored in the iCloud and what they equate to in megabytes or gigabytes.
- Choose Google photos as the destination and select whether you wish to transfer photos, videos, or both. You'll then receive a warning that the transfer may encounter Problems if you do not have sufficient storage space in your Google account.
- Google offers 15Gb on its free tier so if your entire photo library is more than that you may need to pay Google for additional storage space.
- Once you're happy, click continue and you're then asked to Provide your Google account credentials

and allow apple permission to make the transfer.
- Click allow followed by confirm transfer.
- All you have to do now is sit and wait and you can check the status of the transfer by logging in to your privacy settings.

How to transfer data from a blackberry or Windows phone to a Pixel

You cannot use the Quick Switch Adapter on BlackBerry or Windows Phone. However, your Google account on your Pixel will automatically sync any Data that is saved on it after you sign in. Use the steps below to move other data:

- Back up your data on the old phone.
- Install the app phone transfer to your PC.
- Run the Program and connect both phones to the computer.
- Click on restore from backup and choose the backup file on blackberry or Windows storage.
- Select the data you want to move to your new phone and then tap on start transfer.

CHAPTER 3

Start Your Device

To start your Pixel 6 device, press and hold the power button at the side of your phone for a few seconds.

Charge your Pixel phone

Your Pixel phone uses a USB-C cable and you can also charge it wirelessly with Qi- compliant accessories. To charge your phone;

- Plug your USB - C cable into your charging port.
- Then plug the other end into the small power adaptor in your retail box.

- Lastly, plug the end of the adapter into an outlet. Viola! your phone will start charging.
- If you are using a Qi- compliant accessory just place the back of your Pixel device on it.

How To Reboot

Here are three ways that you can use to power off or restart your Google Pixel 6 or 6 Pro

- The first way is a two-key combination. What you want to do is press the power button and the volume up at the same time then go ahead and click power off or restart.
- Another way is to slide down your notifications from the top twice.

You will see the power off button right there. Tap on it and you can power off or restart.

- The last way is to force a restart. You may want to force a restart if maybe the screen is frozen or not unresponsive when you try to power off or restart. To restart, press and hold the power and volume up button until the screen turns black. Let's go and wait for it to boot back up.

Using a Nano SIM Card

Here, I'm going to show you how to insert your SIM card on a Google Pixel phone.

- First, take your sim opening tool. There's one included in the box.
- Then you want to identify the SIM tray on the side and take the tip of the tool and gently push it into the small hole at the side.
- Once it pops out, grab it with your finger and pull the tray out.
- Grab your nano-SIM and your card in a way that it aligns with the edges of the tray. Make sure that the metal contacts are facing done.
- Insert the tray back into its slot and push it in till it snaps in place.

- Turn on your phone and the sim sign should be reading now.

Make Use Of E-sim

If you have already inserted your nano-SIM and you want to use an eSim too, follow these steps;

- Go to settings and click on network & internet.
- Next, click Mobile network and then tap +.
- Select download a sim instead
- When a Prompt asks if you want to use two Sims select yes and wait for your phone to update.
- Once it's done, open the Settings app again and Network & Internet and choose Mobile network.

- Tap on your networks to set your sim preferences.

Connect to Wi-Fi networks on your Pixel phone

In this section, I'm going to show you how to connect to your home wi-fi network on your Google Pixel 6 or 6 Pro. It's very simple

- The first thing is just go ahead and go to your settings app. You can slide up and look for the settings icon and click it.
- Tap Network and internet and then click on Wi-Fi to turn it on
- Once it's on, tap it again and it's going to start looking for all the networks that are in your range
- Find your network name and tap on it.

- Now if yours does not show, go ahead to wherever your modem or router and reset it. Just pull the power plug, wait one minute and plug it back in. Then give it a couple of minutes and come back to the phone and check if your network name is there now.
- Once it's there, go ahead and input your password then tap on connect.
- As soon as it connects, you will see your Wi-Fi bars at the top of the screen and your phone is ready to browse.

How to make The Most of Wi-Fi

If your Google Pixel 6 or 6 Pro phone is having issues connecting to Wi-Fi; here are a few steps to fix the issue.

- Restart your phone
- Disconnect and forget the Wi-Fi network. Then search and pair with it again.
- You can also try resetting your phone to factory settings.
- Finally, access your developer options;
- First, go to your settings apps. Scroll all the way down and tap on System then tap About phone. Scroll down and click developer options 7 times 50 activate it.
- Enter your PIN number if needed then tap the back button twice to go back to System.

- Tap Advanced, then developer options.
- Now scroll down and locate Connected Mac Randomization. Toggle the button to turn it in.
- Then go ahead and turn on your Wi-Fi and see if it connects.

How to connect to mobile networks on a Pixel phone

You can connect your phone to the mobile network by turning it on in your mobile network setting. Your phone's browsing capacity is highly dependent on your service plan and carrier.

- Go to your Settings app.
- Click on Network & internet, and then tap on Mobile network.
- Click Mobile Data to turn it on or off.

Modify the setup of the mobile network

- Go to your Settings app.
- Click on Network & internet, and then tap on Mobile network.
- On the next screen, click on a setting to modify it.

How to use your Pixel 6 phone with any mobile carrier

To use your Pixel phone with a mobile carrier that is not the phone's seller network, you have to get a sim unlocked phone. You can get a sim locked or unlocked phone depending on where you buy it from. Your Pixel phone will work with all major sim Providers.

Acquire and use a sim-unlocked phone

To acquire a sim unlocked phone just order from the Google website. Most of the phones there will already be unlocked.

- Purchase a sim unlocked phone from Google
- Contact your preferred Sim Provider

- Now set up your phone with their service plan.

Possessing a sim-locked phone

If you possess a sim-locked phone, you must be aware that your phone could be sim-locked for up to 2 years. Until the contract ends or the sim Provider removes the lock, you will only be able to get mobile service from them.

To unlock your phone before the end of the 2 years, contact your sim Provider for more information.

Resolve issues linked with the removal of a sim lock

Once the original carrier removes the sim lock your sim should start working immediately. If it doesn't work after that, follow these steps to troubleshoot;

- Connect your phone to a wifi network. (Follow the steps above to connect your phone to WiFi.)
- Check if there are any Android updates available and update them.
- Open your dialer and dial this code: * # * #7465625# * # *.
- Call it and wait for your phone to return to the dial screen. It could take about 2 minutes.
- Now check if you have a mobile connection.

If this step does now work, reset your phone to factory settings. Once your phone has deleted all data on it, set up your phone and follow the on-screen steps.

If this step also does not work, then the last step is for you to contact your mobile carrier.

How to use dual Sims on your Google Pixel phone

With your Pixel 6 or 6 Pro, you can use two Sims; one eSim and one physical nano sim. You also have the choice of deciding which of the sim will be used for calling, messaging, or browsing. It is called the Dual SIM Dual Standby (DSDS).

To find out if eSim and DSDS will work with your mobile carrier, kindly contact them. In previous sections, we have discussed how to utilize a nano-SIM and make use of eSim on your Pixel phone.

How to place a sim card into the phone while it is switched off.

In this section, I am going to show you how to insert your SIM card into your phone.

- Now first off: when you take the phone out of the box and be sure to leave it powered off.
- Next, you're going to want to locate where the SIM card tray is on your phone.
- it's usually on the other side of your phone.

- Now once you find the SIM tray, you're going to need to pop it out.
- Your device will come with the SIM removal tool, please use that.
- Just insert the tool into the small hole on the door itself.
- Go ahead and place your sim on the tray.
- Now just gently insert the SIM tray back into your phone until it snaps into place.

CHAPTER 4

Getting around on your Pixel phone

The Pixel phone comes with different gestures for you to navigate around your phone. To Make your selection,

- Tap your Settings app
- Click on system
- Locate gestures and tap on it
- Then click on system navigation
- Then choose an option either the Gesture navigation, or 3 button navigation.

Quickly change settings on your Pixel phone

With Quick Settings, you can change settings from anywhere on your phone. You can have any setting that you would be changing often, and add it to your quick setting for easy access.

- To open quick settings, swipe down from the top of your screen. Only a few will be visible.
- To see all your quick settings, swipe down again.

Add, remove or move a setting

In this section, I'll be showing you how to rearrange these quick-setting tiles as well as how to add new ones to them.

- Once you expand the quick settings panel down you can see several icons, your avatar picture for your Profile, and then you have a pencil.
- The pencil icon is how to edit the quick settings panel.

- Tap on that pencil and then it will open up the Edit screen. It will be divided into three sections.
- The top section is what is active right now on your quick setting. The second section is what you can add to the active section and the third section is for third-party applications and tiles that just aren't built into the Android system or aren't enabled by default
- To move any tile, you just need to tap and hold and drag it wherever you want it to be.
- To add any tile, tap and drag the icon to "hold and drag to add tiles."
- To remove a tile, hold and drag it to "Drag here to remove."

How to Take a Screenshot Or Record Your Screen On Your Google Pixel Phone

- Go to the screen you want a screenshot
- Press the volume and power button at the same time
- Once it takes the Screenshot it will show a preview at the bottom of the screen.

Using your Pixel 6 to take a snapshot of the current screen and preserve it

To screenshot with your Google Pixel 6 devices;

- Go to the content you want to screenshot and preserve.
- Then, press down the volume and power button at the same time.
- The screen will be captured and it will display a preview of the picture with options to edit, share, save, etc.

How to identify share and edit a Google Pixel screenshot

To identify your screenshot, tap on the preview at the bottom of the screen.

How to access all of your screenshot screen captures

- To find your screenshot, tap on your photos app.
- Click on library and then choose the screenshot folder
- To share your screenshot, tap the share icon.
- To edit it, tap the edit icon.

How to translate a screenshot correctly on your Pixel 6 device

Before you decide to translate a picture, you should understand that you can only translate Hebrew, Chinese, French, German, Korean, Japanese, Portuguese, Italian, Hindi, and Spanish.

To translate a screenshot image;

- Go to your Photos app

- Find the screenshot and tap in the lens icon to translate.

How to record your Google's Pixels screen

To record the screen if your Google Pixel;

- From the top of your home screen, swipe down twice.
- Tap on the screen record icon (it may need to swipe right if it's not in the first quick setting. If it's not there, Tao in edit and drag to your active quick settings).
- Go to the screen you want to record and click on start.
- Your screen will start recording after the countdown finishes.

- When you are done recording, just swipe down and tap on the screen record notification.

Create printouts from applications

You can print from some apps on your Pixel 6 device. All you have to do is add a printer that has access to a mobile network or Wi-Fi.

to enable or disable printing on your phone follow these steps:
- Tap on your settings app
- Click the option "connected devices" and then select "connection preferences" before tapping on "printing."
- On the next screen tap on print, service to enable Leeds, or disable it.

To add a print service your Google Pixel 6:

- Tap on your settings app
- Click the option "connected devices" and then select "connection preferences" before tapping on "printing."
- Tap on the option add service and then enter the information of the printer.

To use a print service on your Google Pixel 6:

- Tap on your settings app
- Click the option "connected devices" and then select "connection preferences" before tapping on "printing."
- Click on the print service.

- To manage your print settings, tap on a printer from the list and click on more.

Some apps do not allow printing, so printing from an app depends on if the app accepts printing. If the app does not accept printing, you can screenshot the screen and print the screenshot.

CHAPTER 5

How to customize your device

You can personalize your screen to your favorite content.

Change wallpaper on your Pixel phone

- Go to the settings menu
- Click on Device and then select display.
- You should see the wallpaper option and now you have access to a couple of options to select from; my photos, live earth, new element, live data, and sky-high.
- Select your preferred image from either folder and it gives you the option of setting it for the home screen or lock screen or both.

- Make your choice and it will automatically set.

How to customize the grid on the home screen

In this section, you are going to learn how to change the grid layout of your home screen and also the style of your icons for the apps.

- Long press right anywhere (a blank spot) on the home screen of your Pixel and then tap on styles and wallpapers.
- It will display a screen where you can change your wallpaper for both the home screen and lock screen. However, click on the style option at the bottom of the screen.

- As you enter into style you will see some choices there and a custom option. If you click the custom option, you can choose the font style you want, and then as you press next you can also choose the icon styles that you want.
- Once you're done choose your preferred color, and then press next and then you can choose the shape of your icons and click on next.
- Once you're done you can go ahead and name it to whatever you want to name it and once, you're done press apply and now it's going to take it into effect immediately.

To set up your grid;

- Go back to the styles and wallpapers
- Click on the grid option to go to your grid setup setting and you don't have many choices here in terms of grid setup.
- You have the default which gives you the ability to squeeze in a lot of apps on your home screen.
- If you're not that type of person you want few apps to show up then choose the 4x4 or 3x3 option.
- If you have difficulty seeing 2x2 is definitely the way to go but that's totally up to you. You can always come back and make changes to your taste.
- Hit the checkmark so that the new changes can go into effect on your home screen.

Add apps, shortcuts, and widgets to your home screen

To add apps to your home screen;
- Swipe up from the bottom of your home screen
- Select the app you want to add, hold it and drag it to your home screen.
- To remove it, hold and drag it to the top of your screen.

To add shortcuts to your home screen:
- Tap, hold and release the app, if it has a shortcut, you will get a drop-down menu
- Click and hold the shortcut and drag it to where you want it then release your hold.

To add a widget to your home screen;

- Click and hold anywhere on your home screen and then tap on the widgets option.
- Pick the one that you want to apply to your home screen.
- Click and hold it and then put it where you want on your home screen.
- To customize it, tap-hold then release to resize it.
- You can also put it on another screen by clicking, holding, and then dragging it to the right or the left.

Monitor screen and display settings on a Pixel phone

- To change your display settings, go to the settings app on your phone.

- Click on the display option.
- Go To the setting you want to change and tap on it.
- If you want to see more options, tap on Advance.

Visibility configuration

- Use fonts to change the size of words on your phone.
- The Display size will make your icons smaller or bigger
- Use the auto-rotate screen option to turn your screen in the direction that you turn your phone.
- With VR mode, you can reduce the blur or flicker on your phone.

Modify the language

- Go to your settings app
- click system and then tap on languages and input.
- Tap add language and select your language of choice.
- Then tap and stay it to the top of the list
- If you want to remove it, tap on more and then click on remove.
- At the top, tap More and then click on Remove.
- Select the language you want to remove and tap delete.

92

CHAPTER 6

Manage screen time with digital wellbeing

You can get information on how often you use your phone or a particular app or even how many times you unlock your phone, on digital wellbeing. It helps you to build a healthy relationship with your device.

To manage your digital wellbeing app you need to search for digital wellbeing from your settings app, then enable the show icon from the list of apps, and then set up your Profile.

- Go to your Settings app.
- Click on the Digital Wellbeing option.
- Tap on show your data under the "your digital wellbeing tool."

Have driving mode turn on automatically on your Pixel phone

You can set Do Not Disturb on your Pixel phone to automatically turn on when you are driving.

- Open your settings app
- Click on the Connected Devices option
- Then select Connection preference and tap on driving mode
- From the next screen, click on behavior.
- If you want to make use of your phone when you are driving, click on Android auto and if you don't want to use your phone, tap on Do not disturb.
- Finally, enable the turn on automatically option.

Establish a driving policy in your Pixel phone

- From your settings app, click on sound and then tap on do not disturb.
- Select the Turn on automatically option and then click on add rule.
- In the next section select driving. Confirm it is enabled at the top of your screen.
- If you want to delete the rule, click on delete.

How to make contactless payments with your Pixel phone

You can make contactless payments at stores that accept tap and pay.

- If you don't already have the Google Pay app, download the app in the Google Play store.

- From your home screen, swipe up to find all your apps, then tap the Google Pay app.
- When you open Google Pay, you can use the same Google account you use for the Google Play store.
- Or if you want to use a different account, you can tap the existing account name and then tap Add another account.
- Once you've chosen an account, tap Continue and add your phone number so you can begin sending and receiving money through Google Pay.
- Then tap Next. You'll receive a verification code at the number you entered.
- Enter the verification code, then tap Next.

- And then choose if you want your contacts to be able to see you on Google Pay.
- You can also choose to earn rewards when you shop with Google Pay, and you can choose to personalize your Google Pay experience.
- To add a card, tap the card icon, then tap credit or debit card. You can take a photo of the card or enter details manually.
- To make purchases in stores, make sure your Pixel phone has NFC turned on and that you have verified your card.
- Now you can make payments with Google Pay on your Pixel phone.

NFC activation (near field communication)

To activate it deactivate NFC on your device

- Go to settings
- Click on connected devices
- Tap on the connection preferences option and click on NFC on the next screen.
- Click the switcher at the side to enable it.

Disabling contactless transaction

To disable contactless transactions on your phone, follow the steps below;

Go to settings
- Click on connected devices
- Tap on the connection preferences option and click on NFC on the next screen.
- Click the switcher at the side of use NFC to disable it.

Find and set up devices near you

To find and set up devices near you, turn on your Bluetooth, notifications, and location.

You can set up any accessory that works with a fast pair (it is often written on their retail box).

- Turn on the device that is not yet set and turn on pairing mode.
- On your phone, you will receive a notification to set up a new device.
- Click in the notification and follow the steps as they appear on your screen.

Allow or disallow notification

You will always receive notifications when there are nearby devices that you can set up. To turn off notifications;

- Open your Settings app.
- Click on Google, then tap in devices and sharing
- In the next screen select the device.

- Then enable or disable Scan for nearby devices.

Resolve configuration issues with devices

If the device is not connecting

- Check if you're close to the device
- Confirm that your Bluetooth and location is turned on
- Check if your mobile network or Wi-Fi network is connected

CHAPTER 7

Use gestures on your Pixel phone

- Swipe down from your home screen to check your notification or to the screen while it is locked.
- Press your power button twice to open the camera
- Press the volume up button and the power button to turn your phone's vibration on
- Turn your phone face down to activate do not disturb mode
- Wave your hand over your phone to skip a song or play the previous song
- Squeeze the bottom half of your phone to activate your Google assistant

Activate or Deactivate gestures

- From your settings app, click on system.
- On the next screen tap on Gestures.
- Then select and change the gesture from the options listed.

Get the most from your Pixel phone battery

You can help your battery to last longer, by taking care of how the battery drains during use.

- Use Adaptive Battery to keep apps you use less often from draining your battery power. Adaptive Battery is turned on by default.

- To turn Adaptive Battery on manually, go to your Settings app and tap Battery.
- Then tap Adaptive preferences and click the Adaptive Battery setting on.
- To help conserve battery, the Battery Saver feature stops apps from running in the background and turns off location services when your screen is off.
- To turn on Battery Saver, swipe down from the top of your screen and then swipe down again to expand the menu.
- Swipe to the side for more options and tap Battery Saver. When you turn on Battery Saver, you can also choose to turn on Extreme Battery Saver.

- To use Extreme Battery Saver, open your phone's Settings app.
- Tap Battery and then Battery Saver.
- Then tap Extreme Battery Saver and then When to use it.
- Now you can choose when Extreme Battery Saver will be enabled.
- You can also choose which apps will still run while Extreme Battery Saver is on.
- When an extreme battery saver is on, the feature will automatically limit apps to only their essential functions.

Other options include:
- Reducing your screen brightness
- Turning off your screen when not in use

- Disabling sound and vibration on your keyboard
- Charging sparingly
- Using the adapter that comes in the phone's retail box to charge the phone

Restriction of apps that consume battery

- Click on battery from your phone's setting screen
- There will be suggestions in the app to restrict, tap the card and then press restrict.

How to make Use of less mobile data with data saver

Data usage is how much data a particular activity like download or app consumes data.

- Swipe from your home screen
- Tap in your settings app
- Click on network and internet
- Then select Data saver from the options
- Tap the switcher to enable it.
- Once activated, the icon will show on your status bar.

How to change your screen color at night on a Pixel phone

- Tap on settings
- Click on display and then select dark theme

- Then tap on schedule and enable the option to turn on from sunset to sunrise.

How to change your screen to night light or amber automatically

- Tap on settings
- Click on display and then select dark theme
- Then tap on schedule and select, "turn on at custom time."
- Go ahead and enter your preferred start and stop time
- Then enable the option to turn on from sunset to sunrise.

CHAPTER 8

How to make and receive phone calls

- Tap on your phone app
- Enter the number you wish to call by tapping the dial pad. Pick a number from your contact by tapping on contacts. Tap on favorites or recent to pick a number from there.
- Click on call.
- When you are done click the red phone button to end the call.
-

Accept or decline a phone call

- To accept a phone call, tap on answer or swipe as instructed on your screen.
- To decline a call, tap dismiss and swipe in the direction your phone indicates.

Check your voicemail

You can check your voicemail messages by calling your voicemail service

- Open your phone app
- Tap on the dial pad
- Touch and hold the 1 key

How to enable transcription or voicemails

- Open your phone app
- Click more options and then select settings.
- From the options tap on voicemail. Then enable voicemail transcription.

Activate donation for voicemail transcription

- Open your phone app
- Click more options and then select settings.
- Click on Voicemail transcription analysis to activate.

How to change call settings

You can change your ringtone, modify the volume, choose if you want your phone to vibrate, etc.

Modify the volume and vibration settings

- Go to your phone's app
- Tap on more, then select settings.
- Click on the sounds & vibration option
- You can change your ringtone, vibration intensity from here.

Modify the text responses

- Go to your phone's app
- Tap on more, then select settings.
- Select Quick responses
- Tap and edit a response on the screen

- Then click on ok to save.

How to block a contact/number

- Click on the three dots at the top of your screen, select Settings.
- Tap on blocked numbers and then select Add a number
- Add the number you want to block
- Tap on block.

How to use caller ID & spam Protection

If your caller ID and spam Protection is on, it will give you information about the person calling you.

Disable or enable caller ID and spam prevention

- To enable caller ID and spam Protection, open your dialer app
- Tap on more and then select setting
- Click on spam and call screen
- Tap on it to enable or disable it.

Enable caller identification announcement

- Open your dialer app
- Click on the three dots and then setting
- Tap on caller id announcement and then activate announce caller ID.
- Select one of the options and close the app once you are done.

How to block and unblock a phone number

- Open up your dialer app
- Tap on recent and you will find all the recent numbers that have called you.
- Assuming the number you wish to block has called you, it will be visible there.
- Press and hold your finger on the number till a list of options displays.
- Click on block and confirm it.
- To unblock tap on the three dots on your dialer app
- Click on settings and select blocked number
- A list of numbers you have blocked will show, click on the one you want to remove and tap on unblock.

How to screen your calls before answering them

- Open your dialer app
- Tap on the three dots on your screen and select settings.
- Then tap on spam and call screen from the listed options
- Enable see caller and spam id before clicking on the call screen
- Tap the types of callers you want to screen below unknown call settings
- Select whether the call should be declined, automatically screen or if it should ring out.

Where is call screen accessible

Call screen is accessible automatically across all Pixel devices. to screen calls manually you have to be in either of these countries; Canada, Italy, Ireland, Japan, Germany, Spain, Australia, US, France, or the UK.

How to use other apps while on call

You can continue your car and use other apps at the same time with the picture in picture mode.

How to utilize picture in picture mode

- Whilst on your call, press the home button
- The call will continue and you can go ahead and open another app

Use Google assistant to make calls on your mobile device.

Google assistant can help you place a call to your friends, family, colleagues, etc. just with your voice command

To place a call just say "Hey Google" followed by the command

- Call (name as saved on your contact)
- Redial

How to use direct my call

Direct my call will show on your screen what an automated voice is saying and menu options available when you call a business number.

It only works in English, for residents in the US, and on the Pixel 6 phone.

How to activate or deactivate direct my calls

- Open the dialer app,
- Tap on the three dots, then click on settings
- Select Direct my call
- Enable or disable direct my call from the next screen.

CHAPTER 9

How to add new contacts from a group conversation to your contact list.

- Open the messages app
- Open the group conversation the person is a part of
- Tap on the three dots on your screen and select details
- Then click on the number you want to add and then tap on add contact

Modify individual notification settings

- Open the messages app
- Open your personal chat with the person
- Tap on the three dots on your screen then tap on details and click notifications from here you

can enable or disable notification for the person and even edit how the notification will display

Send and receive text messages in messages

- Open the messages app
- Select start chat
- Type the name or number you want to send the message to
- Type in your message and press send

How to send photos videos or voice recordings in messages

- Click on the message icon on your home screen
- Select start chat
- That the name or number you want to send a message to

- Click on the image icon beside your chat box
- Tap on the gallery option and go to your desired folder and select the picture or video you want to send
- Click send once you're done

How to Provide your location information

You can send your location to emergency services when you call them using the Emergency location service;

- Open your settings app
- Tap on location then click on location services
- Select the ELS option and then enable or disable the ELS location

CHAPTER 10

How to use applications on your device

From anywhere on your screen swipe up and select the app you want to use. To switch between recent apps, tap on recent if you are using the three navigation or swipe the home navigation to the right if you are not.

How to download applications on your device

- Go to Google play store
- Type in the name of the app you want to download
- Verify if the app is reliable through the ratings and reviews
- Click on install and wait for it to download

Download appropriate apps from third-party sources

- Search for the app you want to download from a third-party website.
- Follow the steps as stated by the source to download.
- Once done tap on the downloaded app.
- Click settings from the message that opens and enable allow from this source.

How to alter the app setting

- Go to your settings app
- Click on apps
- Tap-on see all apps and look for the app that you want to alter its settings
- Play confirmation

- Click on permission
- From the permission, settings tap on allow or disallow

Automatically deactivate unused app permissions

- Go to your settings app
- Click on apps
- Enable Remove permissions and free up space under the unused apps section

How to disable or get rid of apps on your device

- Go to your play store app
- tap on your Profile icon at the top of the screen
- Click the manage apps and devices option

- Then tap on manage from the next screen
- Select the app you want to get rid of and tap on uninstall.

How to disable any Program that came pre-installed on your Pixel 6 device

It is impossible to delete any app that comes pre-installed on your Pixel device. You can, however, disable some of them.

- Go to your settings app
- Click on Apps then tap on all apps
- Go to the app you want to disable, click on it.
- Click on disable at the top of the screen.

CHAPTER 11

How to Protect your device

In the event that your phone is stolen or lost, you can prevent the person from using your phone even if it was formatted. To Protect your phone;

- Add a Google account to your device.
- Set Screen lock

How to find your device

You can find your lost or stolen device through the Android.com/find website or through the Find my device app.

Ascertain the location of your smartphone

To ascertain the location of your phone, your location needs to just be toggled on.

- Go to settings
- Click on location, then enable location.

How to enable the find my device feature

- Go to your settings app
- Tap on security then select find my device
- From there, enable the find my device option

Locate, lock or delete a lost or stolen Pixel device

If your Pixel device was stolen or lost, you can locate, lock or delete it. Find my device will automatically be enabled when you add your Google account to the phone. To find your lost device, your phone should be turned on, the Location should be on, you should have signed in to your Google account. The phone should be connected to the internet via Wi-Fi or mobile network and find my device should be enabled.

How to lock and unlock your device

- Sign in to your Google account on this website android.com/find
- Your lost phone will receive a notification

- From the map on the website, you will see information on the location of the phone.
- The next step is to choose what you want to do. Click on Enable Lock, and Erase if needed
- A list of options will display; secure device, play sound or erase data. Proceed to choose your next action.

Configure screen lock on your Pixel 6 device

Setting screen lock on your Pixel 6 device adds a layer of Protection to your phone. Every time you turn on the display of your phone you will be asked to enter a pin, password, or pattern before you can get access to the phone.

- From your Settings app, tap on security
- Select the kind of screen lock you want to use by clicking on screen lock.
- If you already have one set, it will ask for it before you can pick another one.
- Select the screen lock option you prefer and follow the instructions as they display.

How to unlock your Pixel 6 device using your fingerprint

- Tap on security from your settings app
- Select fingerprint unlock and then follow the instructions on your screen.

- Scan your fingerprint by placing your finger on the sensor

Use your face to log into apps and confirm payment

You can use your face to unlock your device, confirm payments and log into some apps.

- Go to Settings
- Tap on security then click on face unlock
- Enter your pin, pattern, or password
- At the bottom of the screen, click on set up face unlock, agree to the pop-up and then press start
- Fit your face in the frame displayed and then point your nose slowly towards each blue tile

- Tap on done once the scan is complete.

To use your face to log into apps and confirm payments;

- Go to Settings.
- Tap on security then click on face unlock.
- Enter your pin, pattern, or password.
- Enable the App sign-in and Payment option.

How to delete all facial information

- Go to Settings
- Tap on security then click on face unlock
- Enter your pin, pattern, or password
- At the bottom of the screen, click on Delete face date and then press delete

How to disable the facial unlocking feature

- Go to Settings
- Tap on security then click on face unlock
- Enter your pin, pattern, or password
- Disable the unlocking your phone option under the Use face unlock for section.

How to keep your phone unlocked

You can disable screen lock on your phone when you are at home, have the phone in your pocket or the phone is connected to a device that you often use.

- Go to the settings app
- Click on security, then select advanced settings.
- From there press on Smart Lock and enter your pattern, pin, or password.
- Follow the instructions displayed to keep your phone unlocked.

Deactivate Smart lock

- Go to the settings app
- Click on security, then select advanced settings.
- From there press on Smart Lock and enter your pattern, pin, or password.
- Click on On-body detection and disable Use On-body detection.
- Then delete all the set trusted places and devices.

CHAPTER 12

How to change your settings

Quick settings

With Quick Settings, you can change settings from anywhere on your phone. You can have any setting that you would be changing often, and add it to your quick setting for easy access.

Activate quick Settings

- To open quick settings, swipe down from the top of your screen. Only a few will be visible
- To see all your quick settings, swipe down again.

Turn on or off settings

- If you want to turn a setting off, tap on it.

- To see more options regarding that setting, tap and hold it.

Add, delete, or reposition a setting

- Once you expand the quick settings panel down you can see a number of icons, your avatar picture for your Profile, and then you have a pencil.
- The pencil icon is how to edit the quick settings panel.
- Tap on that pencil and then it will open up the Edit screen. It will be divided into three sections.
- The top section is what is active right now on your quick setting. The second section is what you can add to the active section and the third section is for third-party applications and tiles that just

aren't built into the Android system or aren't enabled by default
- To move any tile, you just need to tap and hold, and drag it wherever you want it to be.
- To add any tile, tap and drag the icon to "hold and drag to add tiles."
- To remove a tile, hold and drag it to "Drag here to remove."

How to add or remove Google and other accounts on your device

- Go to your settings app, tap on Account.
- Scroll to the bottom of the list and click on Add account.
- Select the type of account you are adding.
- Tap on Google, if you are adding a Google account
- Choose the personal (POP3 or IMAP) option if you are adding an Apple mail or Microsoft mail.
- Follow the instructions as displayed.

To remove your Google or other accounts;

- Go to your settings app, tap on Account.
- Select the account you will be removing and tap on remove account
- Enter your screen lock and follow the displayed instructions.

Connect your phone to a Google or other account

- Go to your settings app, tap on Account.
- Scroll to the bottom of the list and click on Add account.
- Select the type of account you are adding.
- Tap on Google, if you are adding a Google account

- Choose the personal (POP3 or IMAP) option if you are adding an Apple mail or Microsoft mail.
- Follow the instructions as displayed.

How to delete, switch or add users

- Go to your settings app
- Click on system then select multiple users
- Click on Add user, and then press OK to

Remove any Google or other third-party account from your phone

- Go to your settings app, tap on Account.
- Select the account you will be removing and tap on remove account.
- Enter your screen lock and follow the displayed instructions.

Remove or change users

If you're the owner of the device;

- Go to your settings app
- Click on system then select multiple users
- Besides the user's name, click on settings and then tap in remove user.

If you're not the owner of the device;

- Go to your settings app
- Click on system then select multiple users
- Tap on more and then click on delete (username) from the device.

Change to guest mode on your device

- Tap on User from your quick settings
- Then click on add guest
- If you have an existing guest, you need to delete the previous data so press on Start over
- Or click on continue to keep using the previous guest data

How to create a backup of your Pixel phone's data or restore it

You can backup your data, settings, and phone Settings to your Google account. Once it's backed up, you can restore it to your phone at any time.

You can back up content, data, and settings from your phone to your Google Account. You can restore your backed-up information to your phone.

Activate or deactivate automatic backup

- Go to your Settings app
- Tao on Google then select backup
- Then click on Backup now.

How to back up, restore data and phone settings

- Go to your Settings app
- Tao on Google then select backup
- Then click on Backup now.

Once you've backed up your phone's data, settings, and content. It will automatically sync when you sign in to your Google account on the phone.

How to restore an account from a previous phone to a newly reset phone

- Go to your settings app
- Click on the Google option, then tap on add another account
- Follow the steps displayed on your screen.

How to manage the location settings on your Pixel phone

- Go to your settings app
- Click on location, then tap on location services.
- Click on advanced then enable or disable your location.

Turn on or off your phone's location accuracy

- Go to your settings app
- Click on location, then tap on location services.
- Press on Google Location Accuracy and from there enable or disable Improve Location Accuracy.

How to make your phone conduct a search for nearby networks or devices

- Go to your settings app
- Click on location, then tap on location services.
- Click on Wi-Fi scanning to enable or disable it
- Or two in Bluetooth to enable or disable it.

How to activate or deactivate the emergency location service

- Open your settings app
- Tap on location then click on location services
- Select the ELS option and then enable or disable ELS location

How the emergency locator service functions

The Emergency locator service helps to send your location to emergency services when you call them. It is only available when you call emergency services. It helps them to easily locate you.

Notification and interruption settings

You can mute sound, stop your phone from vibrating, and block visual interruption with Do Not Disturb mode. You can decide what to block or allow.

Quickly disable or enable interruptions

- To quickly disable or reenable interruption, from the top of your home screen, swipe down and then click on the Do Not Disturb icon.

CHAPTER 13

Troubleshooting Your Device

Reboots at random

If your phone keeps restarting, try the following options

- Update your Android system if there is a system update available.
- Check if you have more than 10% of storage available.
- Close all the apps running in the background if you are not using them.
- Reset your phone to factory settings.

Wi-Fi calling will not function Properly

Try these steps if you can't make or receive calls or if your calls keep dropping.

- Make sure you are in an area that has good coverage
- Confirm if your number transfer is still in Progress
- Use your phone's default dialer app
- Enable and disable airplane mode
- Cross-check the number you are calling
- Update Google fi app
- Update your phone Android system
- Restart your phone

Unexpected media pause

If your media keeps pausing unexpectedly try these possible solutions

- Restart your device
- Try clearing the app data and cache
- Update the app is there is an updated version
- Update your phone Android system

Printed in Great Britain
by Amazon